Acknowledgements

Cover: Stuart Franklin/Action Images.

*Photographs: pp. 23, 25 © Allsport UK, London; pp. 2, 6, 10 Hulton Getty, London;
pp. 14, 17, 19 Raymonds Press Agency, Derby.*

Orders: please contact Bookpoint Ltd, 39 Milton Park, Abingdon, Oxon OX14 4TD. Telephone: (44) 01235 400414, Fax: (44) 01235 400454. Lines are open from 9.00–6.00, Monday to Saturday, with a 24 hour message answering service. Email address: orders@bookpoint.co.uk

British Library Cataloguing in Publication Data
A catalogue record for this title is available from The British Library

ISBN 0 340 74737 4

First published 1999
Impression number   10 9 8 7 6 5 4 3 2 1
Year   2004 2003 2002 2001 2000 1999

Copyright © 1999 Andy Croft

All rights reserved. No part of this publication may be reproduced or transmitted in any form or by any means, electronic or mechanical, including photocopy, recording, or any information storage and retrieval system, without permission in writing from the publisher or under licence from the Copyright Licensing Agency Limited. Further details of such licences (for reprographic reproduction) may be obtained from the Copyright Licensing Agency Limited, of 90 Tottenham Court Road, London W1P 9HE.

Typeset by Fakenham Photosetting Ltd, Fakenham, Norfolk.
Printed in Great Britain for Hodder & Stoughton Educational, a division of Hodder Headline Plc, 338 Euston Road, London NW1 3BH by Redwood Books, Trowbridge, Wiltshire.

ER/ 796.334

DERBY COUNTY

Andy Croft

ER/796. 334 R53358L
05.01.2000

Published in association with The Basic Skills Agency

Hodder & Stoughton

A MEMBER OF THE HODDER HEADLINE GROUP

Contents

1 Beginnings

Derbyshire Cricket Club wanted to make money
in the winter.
So they started a football team in 1884
called Derby County.
They played at the cricket club's
Racecourse Ground.
There is a ram on the cricket club badge.
The football club became known as the Rams.
They even played in the cricket club's colours.
Gold, pale blue and chocolate.

In 1895 the club moved to a ground
where people played baseball.
There were some gypsies camping on the field.
They didn't want to leave.
One of the gypsies put a curse on the club.

The 1895 English football team.
Derby's most famous player, Stephen 'Paleface' Bloomer
is seated, second from left.

2 Early Days

The Football League was founded in 1888.
Derby County was a founder member.
They won their first game 6–3 away at Bolton.
It was the highest score of the day.
Derby were top of the table.

A few weeks later Derby were to play
Notts County in the League.
The two teams had also been drawn
to play each other in the FA Cup that day,
so they postponed the League match.
This was the first ever re-arranged match.

Derby played good football.
But they didn't always win.

Stephen 'Paleface' Bloomer was Derby's
most famous player.
He could shoot with both feet.
He played 525 times for Derby
and scored 332 goals.
He was the League's leading scorer
five times in eight years.
He scored 28 times in 23 games for England.

But Derby just couldn't win anything.

Between 1895 and 1909 they played
in eight FA Cup semi-finals.
They played in three finals.
But they couldn't win the cup.
They lost 3–1 to Notts Forest.
They lost 4–1 to Sheffield United.
They were even beaten 6–0 by Bury.

In the old days Derby had some great players
like Jack Barker, Sammy Crooks
and Hughie Gallacher.
Jack Bowers once scored 37 goals
for Derby in one season.
But they just couldn't win anything.

Perhaps the curse was working ...

Billy Steel.

3 Trouble

Nothing seemed to go right for Derby County.

During the Second World War
the Baseball Ground was bombed in an air-raid.

Once the club was fined
for paying players too much.
The directors were suspended
and the manager was banned.

Derby broke the British transfer record
in 1946.
They paid Morton £15,500 for Billy Steel.
In those days clubs were only allowed
to give a new player £10 to sign on.
Derby gave Billy Steel more than this.
The club was fined again.
This time it was the chairman
who was suspended.

They were once fined for asking another player
to come to the club.

They were fined for letting
old-age pensioners into matches
for half price.

They were even fined for paying a player
to write for the match programme.

Derby County have been fined
more than any other club
in the history of the Football League!

4 Success at Last!

After the War people wanted to see
lots of football.
FA Cup ties were played over two games
in 1945–6.
That season Derby won nine FA Cup matches.
They scored 37 FA Cup goals.
It is still a record.

The Rams met Birmingham in the semi-final
at Maine Road.
The game was played on a Wednesday afternoon.
Over 80,000 people saw Derby win!
The Government did not like people
missing work to watch football.
Mid-week afternoon matches
were banned after this.

The Derby County captain, Jack Nicholas,
being carried by his team mates
after their Cup Final victory over Charlton.

Derby met Charlton in the final.
It was Derby's fourth FA Cup Final.
Derby's captain Jack Nicholas asked some gypsies
to lift the curse.
It must have worked!
Raich Carter was brilliant.
Peter Docherty scored once.
Jack Stamps scored twice.
He hit the ball so hard it burst!
Turner scored for Charlton.
But he also scored an own goal.
So Derby won 4–1 after extra time.

At last Derby had won something!

5 Clough and Taylor

By the 1950s the Rams had slipped down
to the Third Division.
Things were so bad they were beaten 6–1
at home in the FA Cup
by non-league Boston United.

In 1957 they climbed back
into the Second Division.
But they were stuck there.
In 1967 Derby were near the bottom
of the Second Division again.

Then two young managers joined the club.
Their names were Brian Clough
and Peter Taylor.
They were a great team.
And they soon built the best team in the country.

Clough and Taylor's team
Colin Todd
Roy MacFarland
Dave Mackay
Bruce Rioch
John McGovern
Archie Gemmill
John Hinton
John O'Hare
Kevin Hector

The Derby County squad
with the Championship trophy in 1972.

Kevin Hector scored 201 goals for Derby
in 581 games.

Two years later Derby were
Second Division Champions!

Three years later they went one better.
Derby were top of the table
at the end of the season.
But Liverpool and Leeds had one match
each to play.
Clough and Taylor took their team
on holiday to Majorca.
They were on a beach
when they heard the results.
Leeds had lost and Liverpool had drawn.
Derby had won the Championship!

The following season Derby reached
the semi-finals of the European Cup.
But they were beaten by Juventus.

That season the Derby chairman fell out
with Brian Clough.
Clough criticised the FA.
The chairman thought the FA
would fine the club again.
He told Clough to stop talking to the press.
So Clough and Taylor resigned.

The semi-finals of the European Cup
in 1973.
Derby were beaten by Juventus.

6 Life After Clough

After managing Notts Forest,
Dave Mackay came back to Derby
as the manager.
He led the team back to the top
in less than two years.
In 1975 Derby were Champions again!
They even beat Real Madrid 4–1 at home
in the European Cup.
But they lost 5–1 away.

The following season they beat Finn Harps 12–0
in the UEFA Cup.
Hector scored five, James three,
George three and Rioch one.

In 1975 Derby played Real Madrid
in the European Cup.

7 More Trouble

The 1970s was Derby's most successful decade.
But the 1980s were a disaster.
The club had eight managers in 18 years.
Soon the Rams were back in the Third Division.
By 1984 they were broke.
The glory days were over.

The club was saved by a millionaire
called Robert Maxwell.
He owned Oxford United.
He also had shares in Reading.
And he tried to buy Watford from Elton John.

Manager Arthur Cox took Derby back
to the First Division in three seasons.
But they didn't stay there long.
Dean Saunders and Mark Wright were sold
to Liverpool.
Derby were relegated again.
Maxwell sold the club.

8 Jim Smith

In 1991 Derby were bought
by Lionel Pickering.
He put £12 million into the club.
He also appointed Jim Smith as manager.
Jim Smith was a very experienced manager.
He had managed Oxford United, QPR
and Newcastle.
His nickname is the 'Bald Eagle'.

In his first season Derby went 20 games
without losing.
In their last game they beat Crystal Palace
to go back up.
Derby were in the Premier League!

Jim Smith has built an amazing team:
Igor Stimac
Dean Sturridge
Lars Bohinen
Stefano Eranio
Mart Poom
Francesco Baiano
Paulo Wanchope
Horace Carbonari

The Rams are now one of the most exciting
teams in the country.

The 'Bald Eagle' Jim Smith
who took Derby into the Premier League.

9 Pride Park

In 1997 the Rams left the Baseball Ground.
It had been their home for over a century.
Many fans were sad to leave.
But they now have a beautiful new stadium.
Pride Park.

Derby fans are proud of their new home.
They are proud of their new team too.
They let in goals.
But they score a lot.
They don't always win.
But they still play good football.

Perhaps the glory days are coming back at last ...

Pride Park – home of Derby County.

If you have enjoyed reading this book, you may be interested in other titles in the *Livewire* series.

Leeds United
West Ham United
Sheffield Wednesday
Blackburn Rovers
Manchester United
Arsenal
Newcastle United